Where do

by Barbara Shook Hazen

illustrated by Ian E Staunton

[To Brack and his baby animals]

▲ Addison-Wesley

bears sleep?

In a den.

An Addisonian Press Book

Text copyright © 1970, by Barbara Shook Hazen
Illustrations copyright © 1970, by Ian Staunton
All rights reserved.
The Addison-Wesley Publishing Company, Inc., Reading, Massachusetts
Library of Congress catalog card number 70-88686
Printed in the United States of America
Second Printing
Single Edition (Reinforced)
SBN 201–02801–8

where do pigs sleep? In a pen.

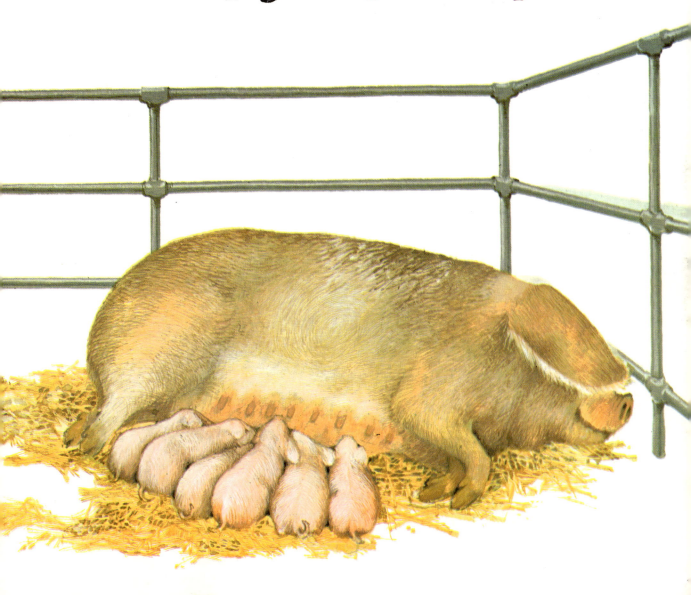

Sheep sleep in a fold when it is cold.

They sleep in the field
when it is hot.

Chickens and
turkeys
rest in a roost.

They like a high
dry spot.

Horses sleep in stalls in stables.

Hoot-owls rest on roof-top gables.

Cats curl in corners,
huddle by doors,

sleep in heaps

on sun-streaked floors

and on the tops
of radiators.

Dogs sniff and stretch
and paw the ground.
Then y a w n
and slowly turn around
before they finally settle down.

They sleep on mats
and cushioned chairs,
beside their masters -
anywhere.

Do **rabbits** *sleep?*

In a nest made of brush
that's lined with grass
and soft fur fluff.

Badgers make their beds in burrows.

Field mice sleep in warm earth furrows.

House mice *sleep in anything soft - on wool*

or in the wall of an attic loft.

Where do hedgehogs sleep? In holes.

So do **weasels**..

So do moles.

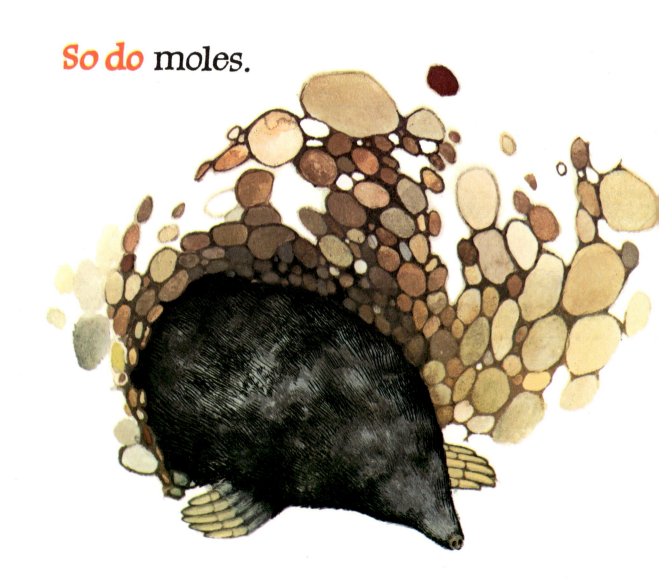

So do
chipmunks.

So do   voles.

An otter takes his reverie
in the mossy bank beside a tree.
A porcupine prefers a bed
of prickly pine beneath his head.

Birds and bats, *what about those?*

Bats sleep on rafters, in orderly rows.

They sleep upside down.
They hang by their toes.

Birds rest in nests.
Some nest in a tree.

Some nest in cliffs
overlooking the sea.

Some in sedges,
some in hedges,

and
some
on ledges
precariously.

Do **snakes** *sleep too?*

Indeed they do.
The bed of a snake
is a hole or pit,

which sometimes is
a very tight fit.

Where does a *ladybug* rest at night?

In the fold of a flower curled up tight,
while tired **fireflies** turn out the light
and on a tree twig say good night.

A **bee** rests her buzz
by a honeycomb cell.
A bee is too busy
to sleep but a spell.

Crickets,   when their song
                        is through
Sleep in a crack in the fireplace flue.

A dragonfly rests
upon a reed.

A mite may slip inside
a seed.

But lucky **you!**
You lay your head
on a pillow soft
on a little boy bed,
with covers to warm you
and tuck you in tight,
your prayers all said
and a small night light,
and Teddy beside you
to keep you from fright,
and Mother and Daddy
to kiss you goodnight.

Goodnight.   Goodnight.

Shhhhhhhhhhhhhhhh.

Sleep tight.